WOUNDED2WONDERFUL

7 Affirmations Towards Healing and Growth

ANGIE MCDONALD

Volume 1

Cover Background Design By: Canva©
Customized Design and Typeset by: Angie McDonald

ISBN: 1984005073
ISBN-13: 978-1984005076
Library of Congress Cataloging-in-Publication Data Available
Library of Congress Control Number: 2019907954

Printed in the United States of America

THE PAIN, EMBARRASSMENT AND OBSCURITY
WERE DESIGNED TO EVOKE YOUR DEEPEST
LEVEL OF EMPATHY AND COMPASSION.
THE PROCESS IS NOT PUNISHMENT, BUT
PREPARATION.
ANGIE MCDONALD

Wounded 2 Wonderful

Volume 1

DEDICATION

Thank you Jesus Christ, for being the Author and Finisher of my Faith. My Alpha and Omega. To the year 2009, particularly the months of July thru November that shaped my Journey and my services to you. To the people during that time, I honor you. Mark Evans, may your soul Rest in Eternal Peace. Thank you for trusting me to be your wife at this pivotal time. Thank you for our daughters Melody and Hannah. Thank you for the courage, faith and compassion you allowed me to experience, and now I'm able to give to others. You've earned your Eternal Reward. To my Second Chance, Darien, I respect your love, support and involvement in helping me to overcome and safely birth this dream. To my additional Miracle, Naomi, thank you for your persistence, will to fight and live. Thank you for the Joy and Peace you've added to our home. I am excited to watch you grow.

To our Butterfly Son, Adonis, our experience together has taught me to value the richness and depth of life, regardless of its length. You were a beautiful boy. Continue to play in the presence of Jesus.

To my Family (Parents, Siblings, Vision Keepers): I salute you. Many of you have helped to guide and nurture me from Birth, and now you witness my continuance into my God-given Destiny.

My COBOAM-GA family, you've embraced and nurtured me into this new level. Your love is indescribable. Thank you.

INTRODUCTION

I want to congratulate you for taking this step! I made sure that I carefully crafted these daily and/or weekly affirmations to stir up the Gift of Healing inside of you! It is waiting for you to begin the unraveling of past and present hurts, disappointments, second-guessing and undervaluing we tend to do as humans.
You can affirm and incorporate these 7 tools interchangeably on a daily or weekly basis. The Choice is Yours!

This is also the guidebook to the Wounded2Wonderful's Online Academy™ 7 Module Course. Here, I will carefully expound on each affirmation, and encourage you to take on each one with bold intention.

Be sure to enroll and be apart of the Journey!
Instagram: @iamangiemcdonald
www.Wounded2Wonderful.com
Email: woundedtowonderful@gmail.com

CONTENTS

How to use this Affirmations Guide

"Wounded2Wonderful: 7 Affirmations Towards Healing & Growth"
is an engaging seven-day and/or seven-week guide empowering you to
"Heal.Grow.Discover."©
Each phase begins with an affirmation and expounded conversation
motivating you to begin Chronicling your Journey towards your
ultimate Gift of Healing.
Using transparency and a realistic approach, this Journaling Guide will
take you through waves of self-actualization, accountability and
expectancy of all that you desire on the other side of Life's challenges.
Feel free to re-apply all concepts to each Challenge as they come, and I
assure that you will learn that you are indeed Wonderfully equipped to
overcome and rise above life's wounds and hurdles.

-Angie McDonald, Board Certified Life Coach, Speaker & Author
Email: woundedtowonderful@gmail.com
Ph: 973-346-2557
Web: www.wounded2wonderful.com / **IG:** @iamangiemcdonald
LinkedIn: LinkedIn.com/in/mrsangiemcdonald

Day / Week 1

Today / This week I will build up a healthy dose of Gratitude for what I have now and work diligently for those things I have yet to achieve. My Ultimate Healing begins with the first step. I am grateful for life, health and the strength to do so.

Today's society can have us feeling so out of touch, unaccomplished, incomplete, ostracised...should I go on? In the era of "right now", with the latest technological developments, at the uttering of our voices, we've become so accustomed to having everything from clothing, food and information right at our fingertips. With that ease of access, also came the war on our self-esteem and image. Our minds have become clouded with what others may look like, have, flaunting or may even be pretending to acquire. Especially with social media, you can feel stuck or left behind with the ever changing trends and quick ways to make thousands or even millions in minutes! Low self esteem has become one of the biggest fights to overcome in the lives of many women, once an exposure to social media (and media in general) has been made. Women are constantly being fed that they're not pretty, skinny, light or attractive enough. This can ultimately result in a life of dissatisfaction with essentially everything about themselves.

What I've mentioned is only the surface of the amount of things we generally are forcefully spoon fed on a constant basis, and expected to gracefully display. The lack of self-esteem has become the greatest blockages to us being able to truly express gratitude naturally. This could be why many of us who have been freed from its relentless grip has found great courage to introduce others to the redemptive power of confidence and self-awareness.

Your When and Your Why?

Take a good look around you. Seriously. I need you to physically stand where you are and take a good in depth look around you. Do you agree you're doing better than most, and greater than some? Does the beauty surrounding your ability to inhale and exhale, along with your cognitive abilities, intelligence and existence presents itself as another indication that you've been gifted the chance to fight another day? The fact that thousands, maybe even millions of people who once said to themselves, "I'll do 'this' tomorrow," unfortunately never experienced their tomorrow. Their lives were cut short, snuffed out, and that idea, vision and life-changing manifestation was thwarted. Even in such tragedies, we who are blessed with life are given stark reminders to live in the Gift called the 'Present'. We are to never give another moment to procrastination, fear and to the harms that may have crippled our innate efforts to just "Be". Sadly, even with the daily reminders of the aforementioned, many still go on without putting any urgency or even priority on fulfilling the dreams and ideas that keep them up at night. This journal is here to help stir up and provoke you to start, or start again.

Use this time to identify and/or activate your 'Why'. Be thankful you were chosen to be the conduit of this amazing Gift that only you have to offer. Be emboldened knowing that you were given an exclusive right to offer your unique gift to your community, generation and world. Have you gotten the gist of *when* to begin? Now, my friend. Right now.

Healing is Where Gratitude Resides.

Gratitude cannot be built on the premise of obtaining things without grit, hard work or experience. Healing is directly related to the practice of uninhibited and intentional gratitude, which is a lesson I learned very early on in my own Journey to Heal.Grow.Discover©. I began my professional services in the Spring of 2016, and before doing so, I had to learn and embrace the art of emphatic intentions and total gratitude. I could not make myself available to you, until I ensured that I was truly thankful for my experiences to this point (the good, very bad and the very, very ugly). I had to write them down and outline them in almost gritty detail. I had to revisit the unique trail of circumstances that took me down Widowhood Way, Single Mother Street and Poverty Place. In reaching my current destination, I pondered and delved into every unsure emotional place that could have harbored any unhealthy or unresolved emotion, and cleaned house thoroughly. This took real courage. However, I had to take my future seriously. Staying in any form of unforgiveness or unresolve was not only going to produce long term problems for me as I attempted to move forward, but it would also plant an unseen seed of delayed healing or further damage as I attempted to bring my services to you. So, as you can see, growing from *Wounded2Wonderful* takes pruning, processing and ideal growth. It had to begin with me, and I am grateful for my ability to heal in areas many of us still struggle with. It is challenging, however it is totally possible and extremely rewarding. Healing is where gratitude resides, and I am here to show you how to get there.

Where You Are Now?

Just like that thumbtack or arrow you'll see on a subway map indicating where you are, I want you to pinpoint yourself to "where" you are now. Where are you on the road of forgiveness, healing, self-discovery and growth? Are you still standing on the platform waiting for the chance or opportunity to get 'there'? Or, is it that you haven't yet come from under the covers of shame, anxiety or guilt? Wherever you are now, rest assured, that with the first step, or thought towards the direction of making a life change for the better, will leave you with no regrets and a passion to pursue all that God has planned for you.

On this first day/week, take the time to assess your 'location'. Whether or not it is ideal, consider my former realizations of you being 'here', alive and well with the *chance* to make progressive steps towards healing, growth and purpose.   Let this be your indication that you indeed are granted   to use yesterday's lessons as today's direction.

CHALLENGE

Challenge yourselves starting right now, with a simple 'thank you.' In November 2016, during my internet talk show at the time "Progressive Movements", I implemented a conversation targeting on having a heart of uninhibited gratitude, regardless of the circumstances at hand. I encouraged my audience to create an atmosphere of thanksgiving, even if it seems there is nothing to give thanks for. I used my own experiences with drastic losses, grieving and financial duress as platforms to still find a way to express gratitude intentionally.

"Gratitude is a seed in the forest of greatness...a tiny representation of what is possible." - Unknown

This message of Gratitude strikes me personally as a major sign of my healing, growth and discovery, as it was the 7th year anniversary of my late husband's passing, birthday and burial in that order. This all took place in the month of November 2009! So if I can look at that experience of losing a spouse, going through exponential material losses and drastic life changes, all through the eyes of Gratitude, you too can learn to give thanks in all things!

So, again I stress, start this day or week with a "thank you". Then begin to build around that utterance with specific things, events, people and successes you've accomplished, even in the *midst* of the pain you might be experiencing. For those things you are striving towards, start to utter phrases of Gratitude for the ability, mental capacity and/or strength to bring those things into fruition. Believe it or not, your words carry enormous power. Your words are powerful enough to either build up and fortify, or to tear down and destroy. You choose.

Use the following space to journal your progress throughout this day or week with the utterances made along with their growing effects.

In all things give thanks... - I Thessalonians 2:13 KJV

Journal your challenges, and your victorious counteractions to them, here:

What Challenged Me?

_____

_____

_____

_____

_____

_____

_____

_____

_____

_____

_____

_____

_____

_____

_____

_____

_____

_____

_____

It's happening, it's really happening!

My Victorious Results!

_____

_____

_____

_____

_____

_____

_____

_____

_____

_____

_____

_____

_____

_____

_____

_____

_____

_____

_____

_____

_____

_____

_____

FACING AND DEALING WITH YOUR OWN
TRUTH IS A SIGN OF GREAT STRENGTH.
WORK FROM THE INSIDE OUT.
ANGIE MCDONALD

DAY / WEEK 2

Today / This week I will awaken and utilize my Gift of

Empathy and Compassion, by paying it forward to someone

who is in need of my Service, Talent or Ministry.

There is growth and healing in giving.

In order for us to grow, we need to learn to extend ourselves. As you may have seen in ecology or geology, if anything wants to grow and gain strength and dexterity, it must first extend its roots wide and deep to the soil around it. The rugged shape and positioning of its roots shows that there seems to have been some resistance in growth and discomfort, until it feels secure in its quite uncomfortable position. As it continues to grow, you'll see that it offers itself completely to the Earth, making itself vulnerable to the elements and space. As it gives of itself, the Earth returns the favor with minerals, nutrients and other essential factors specific to its growth and genetic uniqueness.

You're Built for This!

Your difficulties and mishaps in life are all intricacies to build character, resilience and resolve. This is so hard to comprehend or believe, especially while you're in the midst of the same difficult storms designed to strengthen us. This is where I come in. Having been there, crying the streams of tears, feeling the pangs of grief, loss and degradation, I somehow knew innately that there was more to the pain, the struggle and everything in between. There was a part of me that stood still in the midst of the chaos to 'feel' or listen for the signal that all of what was happening to my children and I, was for a greater purpose. There had to be a reason. There had to be lessons that I had to identify and take note of. There was growing to do, and an extending of my usual capacities to see how beautifully strong and resilient I really am.

The same applies to all of you reading right now. Yes, we've been wounded, forgotten and even 'buried'. However, this is not the time to stay down and not move. Now is the time to open yourself to the Earth and its populace who are in need of your experience, your strength, your gifts or whatever it is you offer that has the capacity to encourage someone to open up and believe again.

CHALLENGE

One will never know if they are a person of Integrity, Moral Compass, Strength, Faith and Character if these attributes were never tested and tried. We must come face to face and contend with our biggest critic: ourselves.

"Adversity introduces a man to himself." - Albert Einstein

Accountability is basically our core responsibility to grow, learn, give, experience and express the matured results of our growth within integral areas of our lives. Practicing accountable living typically can involve the outside interaction from those who may or may not be directly involved in your life, teaching you principles to become more disciplined and refined in your life decisions. However, it does directly involve how you react to their treatment of you, and your intentions to continue towards your growth and ultimate healing.

Use this Day/Week to identify at least one area of your life you believe this current challenge is here to sharpen or strengthen. Take a moment, and write it down below. Right next to that, take a moment to either plan to, or sporadically, bless a person in any capacity.

For example, if you're a singer, why not serenade someone who might be having a not so good day? It could even be a stranger that you want to see smile. If you're a teacher: identify that student who struggles with a certain subject, and give them a boost or provide an additional resource that can help them after school hours. Now don't get me wrong, these examples are some things you probably would do on any given day. However, I'm alluding to the fact you should give when you least feel like it. Make yourself available from an empathetic standpoint. Make an effort to understand the plight of the person in front of you and their struggle, knowing that there might be something you can say, do, or give to raise their hope and faith. This is to remind you, that in the midst of your struggle, we all are experiencing one. It might not be the same exact situation, but the emotion our struggles evoke, typically come from the same place.

So, I hope you catch the gist of what I want you to do, for <u>you</u>! Although we are sidetracked by life's hurdles, life definitely goes on. I want you to be firm in your convictions to still wake up everyday to make continuous strides towards the ideal version of yourself. However, please understand that growing and progressing through life is complete in the cycle of reciprocity. As you cultivate you, be sure to nurture others. That was my awakening. My job is to encourage you to take a few minutes out of your day to do for someone, that will equally bring them and you joy!

"God doesn't need superheroes. He just needs us to be available."
- Angie McDonald

Journal your challenges, and your victorious counteractions to them, here:

What Challenged Me?

_____

_____

_____

_____

_____

_____

_____

_____

_____

_____

_____

_____

_____

_____

_____

_____

_____

_____

_____

_____

It's happening, it's really happening!

My Victorious Results!

_____

_____

_____

_____

_____

_____

_____

_____

_____

_____

_____

_____

_____

_____

_____

_____

_____

_____

_____

_____

_____

_____

_____

_____

AT TIMES REVAMPING REQUIRES GOD TAKING CONTROL OF YOUR LEVEL OF RELEASE, TO BETTER CALIBRATE IT WITH HIS OUTPOURING IN YOUR LIFE.
ANGIE MCDONALD

DAY / WEEK 3

Today / This week I will choose my battles wisely.
*Some conflicts should **only** be met with dignified silence.*
My Healing relies on my self control.

There's no doubt about it, as long as you're alive, conflicts will happen. They come from all angles and from all types of people. No one is exempt: your spouse, family, friends, acquaintances, or even strangers at the market. We're all made differently and uniquely, so your 'norm' might be alien and strange to another individual, regardless of the length of time you've known them. The timing for these conflicts or confrontations to happen are also unexpected and unwarranted. A lot of us may use words that are normal vernacular for yourself in any given moment, but may be a trigger word to someone you're interacting with. Now there are many ways to handle situations. Some require an immediate response to 'nip things in the bud' to effectively quell any rising misconceptions or misunderstandings. Some require careful consideration on how your response should be worded, and being careful not to say something you will regret later. Then there are those verbal 'battles' that you can innately sense will be explosive and toxic. These are the conversations I'm referring to. It's OK to meet these with 'dignified silence.' This is where you would have to carefully weigh the results with the regrets; the pros versus the cons.

Watch it!

To effectively execute proper communication, it is at times imperative to know when to activate careful restraint. This does not mean you've 'lost the battle', or conceded to the war. It simply means your peace of mind means more than being right. Understand that building resilience is knowing when to stand up and speak, or to stand up to walk away.

Carefully assess the environment, consider the results from previous attempts to rectify situations or to talk things through. How did that pan out? Did it feel like time wasted, or as if your energy was drained? If you answered 'yes', then this battle is bigger than you trying to fight it without professional knowledge and protection. By this, I mean having a trained and experienced third party present (therapist, coach, psycho-therapist or pastor). Dignified silence is at times necessary. If you're dealing with someone who has narcissistic tendencies, sociopathic displays of lack of empathy or emotion, or cold and calculated hurtful epithets, then these are the types of discussions you need to respectfully step away from.

Some professionals who believe in consistent and constant confrontations to various conflicts, might have not keenly considered the deep psychological effects that some individuals possess when entering into or attempting to resolve conflict. There are some individuals that are magnets to drama, misunderstandings and arguments. Their need to thrive off of being right, at the expense of you feeling exacerbated after trying to prove your point, innocence or even guilt, will serve no other purpose than to feed their ego, or in many instances, their lack of self esteem.

Your healing depends strongly on your self control. The ability to carefully decipher the kind of energy you entertain is essential whilst on your Journey to Heal.Grow.Discover.©

CHALLENGE

If you find yourself in the midst of a conflict or confrontation, it is imperative that you exercise extreme discretion. Examine it as best as you can to determine if it is deserving of your energy, response and immediate attention. If it is a topic or situation that is necessary and needs urgent resolve, then by all means utilize tact, courtesy and confidence within your response(s). If things begin to seem as if a toxic environment is brewing, I need for you to diffuse the situation with calm reserve. Your healing depends on your ability to initiate self-control and prudence. Cultivating this strength helps you to scale the level of energy certain environments will require of you. Be fluid and transparent with your challenges that revolves around difficult confrontations or conversations. Review, contemplate and gauge all that's involved or at risk. Then move forward with grace and wisdom.

Proverbs 15:1 - A soft answer turneth away wrath: but grievous words stir up anger. KJV

Journal your challenges, and your victorious counteractions to them, here.

What Challenged Me?

_____

_____

_____

_____

_____

_____

_____

_____

_____

_____

_____

_____

_____

_____

_____

_____

_____

_____

_____

It's happening, it's really happening!

My Victorious Results!

_____

_____

_____

_____

_____

_____

_____

_____

_____

_____

_____

_____

_____

_____

_____

_____

_____

_____

_____

_____

_____

_____

DO NOT APOLOGIZE FOR YOUR JOURNEY.
IT WAS DESIGNED WITH YOU IN MIND.
LET AUTHENTICITY BE YOUR NARRATIVE.
ANGIE MCDONALD

Day / Week 4

Today/This Week I will keep believing. I will activate my

Faith, believing that my thoughts are the Substance to the

Evidence I seek!

I seek Healing. I seek Growth.

I seek to Discover all that God has in store for me!

In 2017 I spoke to the Ladies' Ministry at my former home church in Orange, NJ. It was titled "From Evidence to Substance". In that "sermonette" I divulged on our 'trust issues' with God. Not so much as us not trusting Him, but rather our mindset wiring in regards to understanding in actuality that He is trusting us to fulfill our Purpose in the realms of Faith. I encourage you with this affirmation reminding you that God has invested Himself in you!

With His Word, Promises and spoken declarations He's declared you to be:

- Leaders
- Agents of Change
- Physical Expressions of His Sovereignty

Your experiences and giftings are essential to the rest of the World. Your strength is one worth recognizing and worth sharing because it will be a source of healing for those not as strong (according to their belief system). Keep on believing. Keep making steps towards healing and growth.

There is purpose behind your pain! Don't be confused by interpreting it as punishment, or as scourging for past wrongs. We all have lessons to learn, and learning them may not always feel pleasant or be in our favor. However, I encourage you to change your perspective and view your experiences as tools of wisdom. These tools will evidently sharpen your ability to be a prime example of Healing, Growth and

Self-Discovery.

I went on to challenge those women to deeply consider whether or not God has faith in you to manifest and walk in those "thoughts" He has about you, as per *Jeremiah 29 v 11: For I know the thoughts I think towards, saith the Lord, thoughts of peace, and not of evil, to give you an expected end* (KJV).

Now that we're reminded of the awesomeness that has been invested in us, and subsequently expected from us, how do we now embrace the concept of Evidence vs. Substance? How do we now manifest the amazing levels of gifting and service that we can give to the world and community around us? Our healing, growth and discovery can ideally come through our self-realization of who we are in God, in totality: Mind, body and spirit. Your purpose and destiny lies within your recognizance and trust in God's Word concerning You! He had it written with You in mind!

CHALLENGE

Discover and utilize the Power of your words. Especially if those words are graced with God's promises and intentions towards you. Here are a few riveting references to remind you of that power.

- *"Death and life are in the power of the tongue: and they that love it shall eat the fruit thereof." - Proverbs 18:21 KJV*

- *"She openeth her mouth with wisdom; and in her tongue is the law of kindness." - Proverbs 31:26 KJV*
  "I shall not die, but live, and declare the works of the Lord." - Psalms 118:17 KJV

- *How precious to me are your thoughts, O God! How vast is the sum of them? - Psalms 139:17 KJV*

Now that you've gotten the idea of what God knows, how important your words are, and how *awesome* God thinks you are, find your 'voice' utilizing the journaling space to declare some major things over your life. I have found that using the words "I Am", "I Shall" & "I Will", have critically changed the way I see life, and the direction I need for it to take. The trajectory of our lives are determined by the intensity of our faith and belief of all that is greater.

- I AM: affirms who you are
- I SHALL: establishes your authority
- I WILL: confirms your ability

Use the above mentioned declarative precursors in today's/this week's growth Challenge. I am confident you will see a change. Don't forget to make notations of those changes as well!

"And have put on the new self, which is being renewed in knowledge in the image of its Creator." - Colossians 3:10 NIV

Journal your challenges, and your victorious counteractions to them, here.
Also, don't forget to use **I Am, I Shall and/or I Will!*

What Challenged Me?

_____

_____

_____

_____

_____

_____

_____

_____

_____

_____

_____

_____

_____

_____

_____

_____

_____

It's happening, it's really happening!

I Am!

I Shall!

I Will!

My Victorious Results!

_____

_____

_____

_____

_____

_____

_____

_____

_____

_____

_____

_____

_____

_____

_____

_____

_____

_____

_____

_____

_____

_____

_____

YOUR SCARS ARE PROOF THAT YOU SURVIVED.
SHARE YOUR STORY!
ANGIE MCDONALD

Day / Week 5

Today / This Week I will use yesterday's lessons as today's direction.

Experience Teaches Wisdom!

Challenges should be the fuel to our flame of passion and change!

We should see them as opportunities to garner the best ideas, attitudes and habits that will yield the best results. However, as it comes to anything regarding change, it is definitely easier said than done. Learning this revitalizing concept the hard way humbled me. I had a crash course that taught me how important it is to process pain, grief, loss or any challenging feeling. I had to learn how to ask the right questions such as: How will this experience help me to help someone else? What does God want me to learn from this? What narrative to I need to share with the world?

There are a myriad of reasons why we go through certain experiences. They can stem from not so good life decisions, or they can result from drastic changes in our current daily lives in the form of loss (loved one, job, home, car, etc.) that we had no control over. Regardless of the reason(s), one thing remains constant: our ability to responsibly react or respond to these experiences. How we react determines our maturity, willingness to heal, and how well we 'take notes' from the lessons life intends to teach us.

For me, my lessons were to not take my difficult life experiences too personal, or, as a personal vendetta that had my name on it. My bouts with grief, loss and financial hardship weren't exclusively for me to experience the pain these circumstances can bring. The disheartening feelings that can come from losing the one you love, to the very things you worked so hard for can knock the wind out of you. All of these things had me bewildered for a while, but I had to see through the clouds of pain, angst and grief.

As an individual that has been entrusted with certain compassionate capabilities, such as effective listening, counseling or coaching, I have discovered that my life must be a representative of the triumph over the same or similar hurdles I intend to assist you to overcome. I realized that information and education are powerful tools that will help us think of innovative ways to give our circumstances less power in the capacity of worry or insecurity. I instead use these calibrated tools to galvanize and hone in my experiences to intentionally inspire the hearts of those around me and ultimately the world.

CHALLENGE

Read / Network / Research

Without a doubt, using yesterday's lessons as today's direction takes a bit of work. However, the sting associated with those lessons are at times all the push we need to avoid ever going down that path again. Sometimes it requires a bit more than just reminiscing and reflection. Reading up on the challenges endured as well as networking with others who have gone through the same are other pivotal steps to guide you to Heal.Grow.Discover.

Use this day / week to gather knowledge and viable connections to assist you along your healing journey. Regardless of the circumstances, you are not alone! There is someone out there who has gone through similar circumstances and have made bold steps to ensure that a message of hope and healing is available to anyone else facing the same plight. Make a concerted effort to utilize the resources that are easily accessible.

"That horrible experience was not in vain. There were lessons to be learned, growing to do and countless others to inspire. Forge ahead!" - Angie McDonald

Journal your challenges, and your victorious counteractions to them, here.

What Challenged Me?

_____

_____

_____

_____

_____

_____

_____

_____

_____

_____

_____

_____

_____

_____

_____

_____

It's happening, it's really happening!

What New Book or Material Did I Read?

_____

_____

_____

_____

_____

Who Have I Networked With?

_____

_____

_____

_____

_____

What Did I Research?

_____

_____

_____

_____

_____

My Victorious Results!

THE WORLD NEEDS TO EXPERIENCE YOUR
UNIQUENESS THAT CAME FROM THE PAINFUL
PROCESS YOU ENDURED!
ANGIE MCDONALD

Day / Week 6

*Today / This Week I affirm that I am **NOT** my*

circumstance.

It does not own me, neither does it dictate my progress.

I am NOT my circumstance! (Get aggressively intentional about this one!)

Our circumstances has a clever way of making us feel defeated way before the fight is even over. It is typically right at the cusp of breakthrough that the transition becomes the hardest to attain or envision. Our crazy life circumstances will stop at nothing to try and drown us in a consistent wave of complacency, pain and confusion. The feeling of being engulfed of what we see, has the tendency to make it seem harder to embrace the change to come!

However, the old cliche "mind over matter" can take a positive grip on what you've been experiencing as a 'dead end' or 'back against the wall' type of situation. It is with the affirmed thought of knowing that you are the Victor/Winner/Champion over life's challenges and not the victim, is the plot twist we can all insert in our life story.

I confess, I had moments during my first few years of widowhood where I struggled greatly with self-loathing, self-pity and 'crowning' myself as a failure. I believed I failed as a praying wife, because no matter how hard I prayed and fasted, it didn't 'save' my husband. Then I believed I failed as a mother, because there were times I was emotionally unavailable to my daughters, especially around key dates (our wedding anniversary, and of course the dreaded month of November, which was his transition, birthday and funeral in that order). These moments constantly played over and over in my mind, painfully reminding me of the circumstances I found myself in. The realization that I became a 28-year old widow, with 2 small children, left to figure out the rest of my life in a world that has shown me its cruel side, sent me into a wave of anger and regret.

Do you want to know what's funny? I found out that my mind was playing tricks on me! I somehow led myself to believe that I had to own this circumstance. That I had to become the sad, despised widow, who now had to live in pity and self-wallowing regret. I somehow convinced myself that my ineffective prayers left me without a husband, and my daughters without a father. You see how deeply disturbing that thought process was? It absolutely was disturbing, but it was also dominant. It also began to take residence in my thought cycles and how I perceived my future life with my girls. Now I know I'm not the only one who felt those similar feelings of despair, degradation and anger, all brought on by the way we think about ourselves in our current situation. This is why in the beginning of this affirmation chapter, I encouraged you to get aggressively intentional about not only defying, but eliminating that kind of thought process from your mind. It is time to disassociate yourself from thinking that your circumstances define who you are as a person. Let me rather say, these circumstances do not define you, but *refine* you!

See them as ways that will create opportunities for you to contribute your wisdom, insight and strength to many who may see their own life circumstances as unbearable. Envision this as early as possible. Start changing the narrative of your future, with your thoughts stemming from your Now. Repeating words such as "I will never", "I don't even see how", "It's not even possible right now", are actual stallers or even killers of Destiny. Don't sabotage what this lesson is bringing you through, as well as what it is bringing you to! I often say to Clients who are struggling with wrapping their heads around certain life roadblocks that "all the wrong turns brought you to the right place." The detours we experience in life are not designed to be scenic displays of beauty and serene landscapes. These detours are meant to show you the rough patches that we all have to pass through as human beings. Evidently some of us have to pass through some pretty crucial ones in order to reach the beautiful destination we seek.

You may ask 'why' while reading this, or you might experience an epiphany and agree fully. However, the reasons are blatant: to provide you with tools to not only navigate future hurdles with stability and grace, but to also be that nurturing guide to many who feel they aren't quite fit to trod through such rough terrain. Continue the journey from *Wounded 2 Wonderful.*

CHALLENGE

Make Progressive Movements far and away from any negative environment, people and ways of thinking!

Start by outlining the major circumstances that surround you at this moment in time. Be as detailed or concise as you see fit. Ensure that you at least identify the sensitive aspect of what makes this issue so hard to navigate or overcome. Then begin to look at it as a tool for potential growth, and character development. How, you ask? Continuously weigh in the balances, your freedom versus your current emotional restraint. Do you prefer to experience newfound release and freedom from those things that keep you emotionally withdrawn, restrained, and broken? The lessons to be learned are stepping stones towards an amazing future filled with victory, joy and peace. The glorious moments we celebrate in life, would not be as amazing if there weren't some challenging times to teach us how important it is to remain healed, freed and victorious!

Weeping may remain for a night, but rejoicing comes in the morning. - Psalms 30:5 NKJV

Journal your challenges, and your victorious counteractions to them, here.

What Challenged Me?

_____

_____

_____

_____

_____

_____

_____

_____

_____

_____

_____

_____

_____

_____

_____

_____

_____

_____

It's happening, it's really happening!

_____

_____

_____

_____

_____

_____

_____

_____

_____

_____

_____

_____

_____

_____

_____

_____

_____

_____

_____

_____

_____

_____

My Victorious Results!

_____

_____

_____

_____

_____

_____

_____

_____

_____

_____

_____

_____

_____

_____

_____

_____

_____

_____

_____

_____

_____

_____

_____

WHAT GOD HAS GIVEN YOU ORGANICALLY, OTHERS ARE STRUGGLING TO PIECE-MEAL A LACKLUSTER DUPLICATE. WORK WHAT HE'S GIVEN YOU!
ANGIE MCDONALD

DAY / WEEK 7

Today / This Week I understand that in order for me to
experience the Best in all areas of life, I must prioritize and my
mind must be in the state of reception.
As a plant anticipates water and sun, I anticipate my healing,
growth and discovery.

We can all admit to the fact that we want the best that life has to offer: Optimal health, wealth, relationships and the likes. One, some or all of these ideas encapsulate the dreams we all have and aspire to obtain. Some go after the 'Best' consistently, while some may attempt to pursue better and become discouraged, thinking all hope is lost.

In my roller coaster Journey as a widow and single mother of two, I had my significant share of 'stop-and-go' moments in life. While trying to acquire a better way of life for my girls and I, many circumstances presented themselves that slowed down that quest. From unemployment, dire financial strains, wrong relationships and bouts of unfathomable grief, you can say I was a lost and hurt woman. My priorities were out of whack, save alone my responsibility as mother and sole provider for my daughters.

Google Free Image: Swiss Alps

I am extremely grateful that I did have the amazing support of my immediate family and close friends, but the ache of no longer having that cohesive relationship with my husband, caused things to not flow as smoothly as I was accustomed to. That, and missing him dearly, didn't make it any easier.

It wasn't until my eldest daughter, Melody, who at the time was no more than 5 or 6 years old, looked at me one morning and said 'Mommy you're my superhero, and you're going to be famous one day." I recall that this moment happened during our usual morning rush to get them off to school, and myself to work. May I say, I was taken completely by surprise! First of all, I began wondering what would make her say the latter part of her statement, and of course the randomness of it altogether. This was all before I decided to use my experiences to coach, empower, and consult. Her childlike faith in me pushed me in ways I cannot explain, to rid myself of the inconsistencies I used to shape my ways of pursuing things, and to carefully place all responsibilities, goals and aspirations in careful order. After all, my biggest fans were my littlest favorite people.

Clearing my Throat. Now Speak!

After spending some time on being clear about what I need to achieve (both short and long-term), as well as overcome, I began to declare and speak those things into my present and future. I mentally and spiritually opened the door to receive all that is good, worthy, beneficial and blessed. It was at this realization, I became engulfed with passion, and a deeper sense to really discover who I've been called to be.

I'll tell you where it happened: in August 2014, on the beach in Jamaica. I had taken my girls as our first "new-family" international getaway. Melody, was requested to be a flower girl in my beautiful cousin's wedding. I then used this opportunity to intentionally make this our time to enjoy our new lives at an all-inclusive resort. I had already purposely planned two intermittent "mommy days" out of the seven, where I would relish in all the amenities the resort had to offer: spa treatments, water aerobics, sightseeing, and of course my absolute favorite, relaxing on the beach! Water is my all time favorite scenery to enjoy, reflect and to clear my head. It's also a thousand times better if it's tropical, blue and involves sand. I specifically remember that on my second mommy day, I lay there on the beach with an intention to focus on the waves. Thankfully it wasn't at all crowded that day, and I had a clear view of the steady flow of the waves ebbing and flowing.

It was in that beautiful moment I uttered these words: "Lord as the waves flows away from me, I release any and all negative things that have been harboring my healing and progress. Lord, as the waves ebb towards the shore, I receive and accept every blessing, good thing, and open door that You have set before me. I receive my healing, my new life, and the plans You have for me. Amen." It was this prayer that broke the constraints of agonizing grief and the 'stuck' feelings I've been battling for so long. I saw in those waves what I should have been doing the entire time. I should have been in a steady rhythm of ebb and flow. I should have allowed myself to grieve my loss without apology. I should have still believed that there were no regrets during the entire time I realized that I was losing my dear husband. I should have forgiven myself for not being present in the moments that God was showing me the beautiful plans He has for my girls and I.

I encourage you to remain in a steady flow of reception. No longer see your hurts, halts, and setbacks as ways to thwart you, or keep you subjected to them. You should now see them as seeds planted that will soon sprout and blossom into bountiful bouquets of resiliency, God's promises for your life, and for the countless lives you are ordained to inspire.

CHALLENGE

Instead of asking yourself 'why me', look at your circumstances as 'what is this situation trying to teach me?' Seriously consider all the vantage points that our life lessons can actually inspire us to relay messages of healing, growth and discovery to a global audience of eager seekers of wholeness and purpose.

As you close out this week or day with this interactive Affirmations Journal, I want you to understand and grasp a few things.

1. The power of the pen is indeed a force to be reckoned with. Seeing your thoughts, challenges and ideas in front of you will bring about a sense of heightened awareness that Purpose is calling you, and that you need to answer by taking the necessary steps.

2. You were not simply picked on by God and He is not laughing at your struggles. What is happening is an unusual orchestration of Greatness, Boldness & Clarity. It is the ending of

generational curses and disappointments. It signifies the dismantling of mental and emotional strongholds that held you hostage for longer than you would have liked.

3. Please understand that although not all greatness is birthed from struggle, it is your challenges that come to make you stronger, resilient and affirmed. You have to be inclined to see the Hand of God in the things that were brought about to enlighten, empower and encourage you.

"Dance Fearlessly to Your Own Rhythm." - Angie McDonald

Journal your challenges, and your victorious counteractions to them, here.

What Challenged Me?

_____

_____

_____

_____

_____

_____

_____

_____

_____

_____

_____

_____

_____

_____

_____

_____

_____

_____

It's happening, it's really happening!

_____

_____

_____

_____

_____

_____

_____

_____

_____

_____

_____

_____

_____

_____

_____

_____

_____

_____

_____

_____

_____

_____

My Victorious Results!

_____

_____

_____

_____

_____

_____

_____

_____

_____

_____

_____

_____

_____

_____

_____

_____

_____

_____

_____

_____

_____

I AM EVER STRENGTHENED BY AN
UNCONTESTED FORCE.
HIS POWER IS UNDENIABLE, AND MY FAITH IN
HIM ENDOWS ME WITH LOVE, POWER AND A
FOCUSED MIND.
GIVING UP IS NOT AN OPTION.
FORWARD STILL!
ANGIE MCDONALD

THIS PAGE INTENTIONALLY LEFT BLANK.

Bonus Chapter
"Get Ready, Set, Grow!"

(From the upcoming biographical summary entitled "Widow2Wife: The Pain, The Journey, The Miracle")

Reflecting on the times early on in Widowhood, I felt God had a vendetta against me. A very personal one.

Someone close to me, in the heat of a disagreement, said I deserved "it" and I started to believe it. I started to believe that I was cursed for some unknown or unconfessed wrongs that allowed me to now experience the perils associated with death, disenfranchisement and loss. From that arose a self-acclaimed responsibility to walk in that guise of shame brought on by my sins. I set out to pretty much roll with the punches that this new life consistently brought my way. My willingness to rise above and beat the constant feeling of emptiness and grief was on pause. I often felt that verbal rebuke justified that pause, and I decided to own it, until I felt I had 'served my time.'

That statement eventually paralyzed me emotionally and numbed me spiritually. I kept all of that in, all while unraveling mentally.

It was also at this time my ability to heal from my loss was put on an undetermined hiatus. My roots of all that I knew regarding spiritual sustenance were choking and slowly dying.

There were hardly any experienced and empathetic words of encouragement, and if there were, they were void of a real connection to my specific circumstance. This reality sent me further into a state of accepting the fact that I was all alone in this, and I was the one who had to bring me out of this abyss of pain and complete listlessness.

I had hoped that this one instance of having something hurtful and insensitive said to me would be a one-off situation. Instead I became the famed poster child of Obscurity, Rebuke and Shame. I felt myself slowly shrinking into a corner away from family, social events, friends, career moves and anything that involved human contact that resulted in togetherness, happy times and even growth. This was also due to the reality of my very own inability of how to deal with me, or how to handle whenever my mood suddenly switched from happy and engaging to somber and withdrawn. No one knew that anything could have triggered that change: seeing a couple interact with each other, a child playing with or being held by their father, noticing a beautiful wedding band on a woman's finger, or simply anything that reminded me of my life that was now an aching memory. I could not blame them one bit, because I didn't even know how to handle myself when this happened. So, in order for me to make it no one's problem but mine, I voluntarily secluded myself to save everyone else the headache.

Jolted!

One day, one of my sisters visited me at home and said something to me that made me very angry, yet so very awakened. "Do not get comfortable with the idea of loss. Right now it seems that you are." Wait a minute! Excuse me!?

She repeated it, and started to name the things that I lost: my husband, my belongings (that were either given away, or sold with a promise to pay and never compensated for), my property management client contracts that my late husband and I carefully garnered and grew, my luxury car that I had to voluntarily repossess, and the list went on. This particular sister, out of the 3, is the one known to be the 'fire starter', the one to have us thinking big, challenging our business potential and gifting, and the one known with the least filter on her idea of things. For this I've learned to love and respect her more, simply because she stated her claim, with no sugar, straight, no chaser. I was put into a position where I HAD to think objectively about where I was at during that moment, and what I needed to do to get to the next level, which was OUT of the slump I put myself in. This is when the aggressive progression kicked in. I thought about my girls, who were amazingly well behaved and balanced, and who graciously loved me unconditionally while Mommy was figuring this thing out. I reflected on the deep conversations I had with my late husband on where we saw ourselves, and the life we were planning on providing our children. Then I thought about my present state, and how my family (although it was hard for them to understand) rallied around me and supported me as best as they could. I had an amazing support system, and a praying mother, so I literally was ready to break out of this self-destructing shell and face my demons head on.

It was during this uncomfortable time in my life, I came to the conclusion that there was no way I could Grow if I had made stagnancy my friend.

<u>Wounded2Wonderful Lesson Learned:</u>
*I've gone from a place of pity to prosperity. Not only in the financial sense, but emotionally & spiritually. This is where Growth is imminent. - **Angie McDonald***

Dig Deep!

*"No magic potions, no fairy dust, no one to do it for you. Just me. I will push you. I will show you how to put one determined foot in front of the other. That's what I will do. I am inside you, I am called your inner strength. dig deep down and find me". - **Unknown***

Like many of us during our times of transition in life, I was still trying to find my authentic self during this low point. The level of discomfort I explained earlier held me in contempt until I could firmly identify who I really was after this major blow of Widowhood and loss. I became engaged in diving in to find ways to center my focus and tap into my 'well' of purpose and destiny. To think I had allowed the stench of stagnancy to run amok in my life, made me feel ashamed. I then had to reposition that resulting feeling from shame to enlightenment. I had to learn that all of this could have only brought something out of me that wasn't there before, or that I allowed to lay dormant.

Was this easy? It absolutely was not! It took grit, work, consistency and an intention to see myself in the state of deliverance and wholeness that God flashed before my eyes. So, knowing all that was at risk if I delayed any further, I began to dig deep.

In acknowledging the work that it was going to take, I had to learn to dull the negative voices that so often plagued my thoughts: all that I lost, the feeling that I took 300 steps backwards in life when I relocated back to our family's home up north, and let's not forget the vulnerabilities I had when I 'attempted' to re-enter the dating scene. I believe if I hadn't taken that intentional step to no longer let those feelings dictate my every move, I would have been defeated and **still** in a bitter and broken state of mind. I'm also pretty sure I wouldn't have been able to receive my second chance at love and life with my current family and loving husband.

The power of self-discovery, afforded me the priceless opportunity to relay to you the heavy importance of Digging Deep.

This, and everything I present to you, always has a biblical representation. It is in the Scriptures I found the need to resolve the insecurities I fashioned during the early stages of my Widowhood journey. In the New Testament Scripture Matthew 7: 24-25, where Jesus spoke about the house was founded upon the rock. The storm came and the floods came. Every element that was designed to throw that house off of its foundation, and its core, could not happen, because it was founded upon the rock.

Speaking of rocks, I often talk about us hitting rock bottom. Many of us can say we've been there at one point in our lives. Pretty much everything about that experience is normally negative and nothing to write home about. The way we felt, the thoughts we had, the way others treated us couldn't have made the term 'rock bottom' more true. However, it was in my moments of feeling utterly depleted, I learned a major lesson. I learned that in actuality, it is the absolute best place we can ever be. It is at that place, where the only direction we can go from there is up. You're at your foundation, your core. You're able to see and observe all the ingredients necessary to grow. You're seeing the dark places, and not so great things about yourself that requires change and elevation. So as you elevate and grow, you will cultivate a true and sincere appreciation for that space you may have deemed as 'rock bottom'. That horrible place you think you were in, I would like for you to see it as your place of cultivation and germination.

Seeds that bare fruit and greenery are supposed to be planted in the darkest, most isolated and uncomfortable of environments. For the best results, some may have to be fertilized with manure, which normally has an interesting smell.

It also requires water, and the constant presence of elements that will make it feel overwhelmed and under pressure. However, please understand if you see what these elements are there to do, you'll see the common factor amongst them all: to give and sustain life.

In order to dig deep, there is a requirement of solitude, obscurity and separation. This brings one to a place of self introspection: The act of turning the light inwards, to reflect and observe where your Life's Compass is aiming towards and where it needs to be. There are times we will need to have the necessary conversations with God and moments of awareness with yourself to actively engage with Purpose, which is indeed God's plan.

So it was in this dark, uncomfortable and messy place during my Widowhood, I found purpose and all the essential tools to grow from that place called rock bottom. I saw my late husband's illness and death as the seeds that were planted for the greater good. Somehow God saw it fit for me to tend to that garden while I was also being planted. I was being prepared, sheltered and nurtured for the long road ahead, for the numerous interactions I would have to make with thousands of people, encouraging them to

Heal.Grow.Discover and grow from Wounded 2 Wonderful.

So get ready. Set. Grow!

BELIEVE IN YOURSELF WITH THE STRONGEST OF CONVICTION.
ANGIE MCDONALD

Wounded2Wonderful:
7 Affirmations Towards Healing & Growth

Volume 1

Affirmations Summary

Here's a recap of the Seven Affirmations that can be interchanged daily and/or weekly. Use and reuse them as much as you'd like to secure access to your level of breakthrough and fulfillment. Create an atmosphere of anticipation and willingness to see yourself at the pinnacle of Purpose. The following pages are to help you chronicle new life events or challenges, and your reactions to them.

1. *Today / This week I will build up a healthy dose of Gratitude for what I have now and work diligently for those things I have yet to achieve. My Ultimate Healing begins with the first step. I am grateful for life, health and strength to do so.*

2. *Today / This week I will awaken and utilize my Gift of Empathy and Compassion, by paying it forward to someone who is in need of my Service, Talent or Ministry. There is growth and healing in giving.*

3. *Today / This week I will choose my battles wisely. Some conflicts should **only** be met with dignified silence. My Healing relies on my self control.*

4. *Today/This Week I will keep believing. I will activate my Faith, believing that my thoughts are the Substance to the Evidence I seek! I seek Healing. I seek Growth. I seek to Discover all that God has in store for me!*

5. *Today / This Week I will use yesterday's lessons as today's direction. Experience Teaches Wisdom!*

6. *Today / This Week I affirm that I am* **NOT** *my circumstance. It does not own me, neither does it dictate my progress.*

7. *Today / This Week I understand that in order for me to experience the Best in all areas of life, I must prioritize and my mind must be in the state of reception. As a plant anticipates water and sun, I anticipate my healing, growth and discovery.*

Day / Week 1: What Challenged Me?

It's happening, it's really happening!

My Victorious Results!

_____

_____

_____

_____

_____

_____

_____

_____

_____

_____

_____

_____

_____

_____

_____

_____

_____

_____

_____

_____

_____

_____

Day / Week 2: What Challenged Me?

_____

_____

_____

_____

_____

_____

_____

_____

_____

_____

_____

_____

_____

_____

_____

_____

_____

_____

_____

_____

_____

_____

It's happening, it's really happening!

_____

_____

_____

_____

_____

_____

_____

_____

_____

_____

_____

_____

_____

_____

_____

_____

_____

_____

_____

_____

My Victorious Results!

Day / Week 3: What Challenged Me?

_____

_____

_____

_____

_____

_____

_____

_____

_____

_____

_____

_____

_____

_____

_____

_____

_____

_____

_____

_____

It's happening, it's really happening!

_____

_____

_____

_____

_____

_____

_____

_____

_____

_____

_____

_____

_____

_____

_____

_____

_____

_____

_____

My Victorious Results!

_____

_____

_____

_____

_____

_____

_____

_____

_____

_____

_____

_____

_____

_____

_____

_____

_____

_____

_____

_____

_____

_____

_____

_____

Day / Week 4: What Challenged Me?

I Am...

_____

_____

_____

_____

_____

_____

I Shall...

_____

_____

_____

_____

_____

I Will...

_____

_____

_____

_____

_____

_____

It's happening, it's really happening!

_____

_____

_____

_____

_____

_____

_____

_____

_____

_____

_____

_____

_____

_____

_____

_____

_____

_____

_____

My Victorious Results!

Day / Week 5: What Challenged Me?

What New Book or Material Did I Read?

_____

_____

_____

_____

_____

_____

Who Have I Networked With?

_____

_____

_____

_____

_____

_____

What Did I Research?

_____

_____

_____

_____

_____

_____

It's happening, it's really happening!

_____

_____

_____

_____

_____

_____

_____

_____

_____

_____

_____

_____

_____

_____

_____

_____

_____

_____

_____

My Victorious Results!

_____

_____

_____

_____

_____

_____

_____

_____

_____

_____

_____

_____

_____

_____

_____

_____

_____

_____

_____

_____

_____

Day / Week 6: What Challenged Me?

It's happening, it's really happening!

_____

_____

_____

_____

_____

_____

_____

_____

_____

_____

_____

_____

_____

_____

_____

_____

_____

_____

_____

_____

_____

My Victorious Results!

Day / Week 7: What Challenged Me?

_____

_____

_____

_____

_____

_____

_____

_____

_____

_____

_____

_____

_____

_____

_____

_____

_____

_____

_____

_____

_____

It's happening, it's really happening!

My Victorious Results!

_____

_____

_____

_____

_____

_____

_____

_____

_____

_____

_____

_____

_____

_____

_____

_____

_____

_____

_____

_____

_____

_____

_____

SEE, THE FORMER THINGS HAVE TAKEN PLACE, AND NEW THINGS I DECLARE; BEFORE THEY SPRING INTO BEING I ANNOUNCE THEM TO YOU.
ISAIAH 42:9 NIV

HEAL.GROW.DISCOVER.©

ABOUT THE AUTHOR

Mrs. Angie McDonald, CEO of iAM Consulting LLC and Wounded2Wonderful Coaching, provides collaborative expertise in assisting, training, optimizing and preparing our underserved, at-risk and immigrant communities through various motivational and professional efforts. Her professional expertise spanning 20 years, and real-life experiences allows her to have an affinity with those who are aware of their calling, profession, and purpose, but are thwarted by circumstances (unforeseen or poorly avoided), lack of resources and information. Angie's motivational, empathetic, and positive stance provides all whom she engages, with the positivism and resource tools needed to pursue their ultimate goals.

Via Wounded2Wonderful Coaching, Angie is a Board Certified Grief Support and Transitional Life Coach. Her personal experiences with Widowhood at a young age, extreme loss and emotional disparity has afforded her the first-hand ability to turn her challenges into opportunities of offering hope, information and insight towards a new and rewarding life after losing it all. In this capacity, she provides intentional, self-discovery tools to assist anyone who has experienced loss of a loved one, a way of life and various life challenges. Her transitional aspect provides supportive and insightful strategies to make the next level most rewarding.

Angie's Coaching motto is: "Let us grow from Wounded2Wonderful."

Wounded2Wonderful Coaching, is a safe haven of affirmations and dialogue provoking topics to identify our Journeys, Transitions and everything in between.
My experiences taught me the Art of Empathy, and how to be sensitive and responsive to the "core needs" of intelligent souls who were blindsided, thwarted or distracted by life's circumstances.
My Purpose is to encourage you to continue your Journey, engage in your Transition and possess your Destiny!
"You can do this, and I can help!"
Coach Angie McDonald
Life Coach (Grief Support & Transition) | Consultant | Empowerment Strategist | Speaker

For Inquiries, Coaching and Speaking Engagements:
Website: www.wounded2wonderful.com
Facebook: Facebook.com/iamw2w
Instagram: @iamangiemcdonald
LinkedIn: @mrsangiemcdonald
Twitter: @i_amconsulting
Email: woundedtowonderful@gmail.com
Ph: (973)346-2557

Made in the USA
San Bernardino, CA
08 May 2020